WILD and WISE

A legacy journal for the real spiritual lives of men

Introduction to Wild and Wise

The male journey is filled with endless challenges that call for a healthy interplay between wild and wisdom energy. When wild energy dominates, then the possibility for extreme risk taking, self-destructive behavior and danger takes over. When wisdom energy dominates, then there is a tendency to over protect, play it safe and avoid adventure.

We have many great examples of men who, in spite of their self-doubt and missteps, were able to hold the tension between wild and wise energy in balance and changed the world for the good. Jesus, Mahatma Gandhi, Nelson Mandela, Martin Luther King, Oscar Romeo all brought about great spiritual and social change by resisting the urges to choose violence or extreme passivity.

This journal contains 38 meditations that reflect on the challenges and choices that shape a man's spiritual life. How he uses wild and wisdom energy determines the kind of impact he has on his world and to what degree he is aware of his true self, his God-self.

A Man's Spiritual Legacy Journal

I still remember the conversation I had with a woman I worked with many years ago when she described her husband as not being very religious. She told me that he would much rather work in his garden than go to church.

I responded that her husband may not be religious but without knowing it, his passion for creating a beautiful garden made him very spiritual. This distinction between spiritual and religious can go a long way to help us understand the real spiritual lives of men.

All men are spiritual but not necessarily religious.

- Two-thirds of U.S. adults (65%) describe themselves as religious (either in addition to being spiritual or not). Nearly one-in-five say they are spiritual but not religious (18%), and about one-in-six say they are neither religious nor spiritual (15%).

- In every country, net losses for Christians are accompanied by net gains for the share of adults who say they have no religion. College-educated people, younger adults and men are more likely than others to say they are now religiously unaffiliated after having been raised Christian.

Whether a man considers himself religious, that is, church going or not, all men (all humans), in the broadest definition of the word, have a spirituality. Pretty much everything we do and are every day, in some way impacts our spirits in positive or negative ways.

All men have spiritual hungers but very often don't call them that.

- What is it about Sturgis, South Dakota, that draws 3 to 5 hundred thousand bikers, mostly men, to gather for a week of partying and hanging out together every summer?

- What is it that draws 10,000 men to a frozen lake in northern Minnesota to sit with fishing poles around holes in the ice in sub-zero temperatures?

- What is it about being in a deer stand quietly staring into the woods for endless hours waiting for a deer to show up?

- What is it that draws men who have served in Iraq or Afghanistan want to return so they can be with the men they served with?

Throughout our lives, often without knowing it, we seek out experiences that impact our spirits in some way.

What does it mean to be spiritual?

The healthy male spiritual journey consists of a gradual awakening to experiences of wonder and encounters with life's mysteries that give his life purpose and meaning. It is his learning to be attentive to his deepest inner hunger to touch the sacred in the events of daily life. Over time he discovers that by surrendering to the source of life he will be transformed and live with an inner knowing that he is connected to and is in service to all of creation.

Too often because many men are indifferent towards, or have outright rejected, organized religion, they judge themselves or are judged by the system to not be spiritual. In fact, we men are hard wired by our Creator to search the realm of spirit for connections that give our lives meaning and direction.

Even though we often get lost on the journey or get seriously sidetracked because of unresolved struggles, anxiety and pain, or just being too distracted, we are always being pulled forward by the great Mystery to get on track and to go deeper!

"One of the best-kept secrets of our culture is that many men are deeply spiritual and care deeply about their spiritual life. It is a secret, because it is hidden sometimes even from the men themselves!"

Mathew Fox

"Just as a candle cannot burn without fire, men cannot live without a spiritual life."

The Buddha

Every man has a spiritual legacy, a history of his searching for meaning, purpose and encounters with life's mysteries. Whether conscious or unconscious, these experiences reflect the shape of a man's soul and the lasting imprint he leaves on those he loves and the world around him.

This men's journal is designed to help men reflect consciously on their spiritual journey, to record their experiences in written form for themselves and, if they choose, for those who have shared their journey.

Legacy Journal suggestions

There are several different ways you could use this journal.

- Use it as a visual meditation by sitting in the quiet or with some music in the background. Just scroll through the pages at your own pace and let the quotes and images speak to you. Be aware of any feelings and thoughts that surface. The more you are able to get to your gut feelings and out of your head, the better.

- Use it as a journal. Listen to the feelings and thoughts that are stirred up from each reflection page. Then use the questions for each page to focus your thoughts and write down what comes into your consciousness. Consider answering the questions as a work in progress. They could be answered over a few days, or several weeks or even over the course of many years. There is no 'right way' to do this. You may choose not to answer some of the questions and possibly add your own observations.

- Remember, the purpose of this legacy journal is to raise awareness of your true identity as a spiritual being. Who you are on this planet as a spiritually alive man is what will have the biggest impact on the people you love and the world around you.

- You also may want to decide if this journal is just for yourself or if you want others to see it at some point.

1 The persistent, and sometimes misguided, male spiritual quest.

"Many men go fishing all of their lives without knowing that it is not fish they are after."

Henry David Thoreau

1. Describe some of the places and activities in nature where you felt most alive as a child and what it is about those experiences you enjoyed the most. e.g. activities with your family, exploring, playing with neighbors, swimming, fishing, biking, camping, camp fires, working with dad, sports, star gazing, sledding, ice skating, etc.

2. Describe some of the places and activities in nature where you feel most alive as an adult and what it is about those experiences that you enjoy the most — sports, gardening, family gatherings, adventures alone and with friends, camping, road trips, going for walks, running, biking, star gazing, etc.

"The spirituality of the earth is more than a slogan. It is an invitation to initiation, to the death of what we have been and the birth of something new."

David Spangler

1. As a child what were some experiences that activated your sense of wonder?

2. Where and with whom did you most often play with as a child?

3. What kinds of things were you most curious about and made you wonder about as a child?

4. Picture yourself as a child playing somewhere in nature and write a few words to that younger you from where you are now as an adult.

"The mass of men lead lives of quiet desperation."

Henry David Thoreau

"This illustrates that one's biological father is seldom the initiator of the son. It is always another special man who must guide the boy into manhood, from wildness to wisdom."

Richard Rohr

1. As a child, who were the key men and heroes in your life who helped shape your image of what it means to be a male?

2. What were some of the qualities, beliefs, and values that these men reflected?

    a. Qualities

    b. Beliefs

    c. Values

3. As a child, other than your father, what male in your life was a favorite and why?

4. As a child, what messages and images from TV, movies, cartoons and other media impacted your understanding of what it means to be male?

"If you are a young man and are not being admired by an older man, you are being hurt. How many of you in the past two weeks admired a younger man and told him so?"

Robert Moore

1. Who were the older men in your childhood years who blessed you? By the time they spent with you, the way they showed you approval with a look, the way they showed you physical affection, and the way they shared their wisdom and knowledge with you?

2. Who have been the men in your adult life who have blessed you? By the time they spent with you, the way they showed you approval with a look, the way they showed you physical affection, and the way they shared their wisdom and knowledge with you?

3. Who are the younger men in your life that you mentor and regularly bless with your time and approval?

4. Who are some of the younger men and boys you encounter regularly that you will commit to blessing and showing your approval in some way?

"When a father and son do spend long hours together, which some fathers and sons still do, we could say that a substance almost like food passes from the older body to the younger."

Robert Bly

"From day one, deep in his un-conscious, the young boy looks to his father and other significant men in his life and asks the question: 'Is it good that I am here?' How that question gets answered will profoundly impact the rest of his life."

Steve Robach

1. Describe how your father, or a father like figure, blessed you as a child and teen.

    a. Things he said to you.

    b. A look he gave you.

    c. By physical contact in some way.

    d. How he spoke to others about you.

    e. By the amount of time he spent with you doing.

    f. By the things he taught you.

    g. By the adventures he took you on.

2. What qualities and life lessons did you learn from your dad, or a father like figure, that you integrated into your own life?

3. Given that most men did not receive a full allotment of father blessings, write a letter to your father in this space describing any sense of loss you have because of a lack of blessings and also appreciation for any forms of blessings that you did receive from him, and include any sense of forgiveness and gratitude you feel towards him.

"Not receiving a blessing from your father is an injury...Not seeing your father when you were small, never being with him, having a remote father, an absent father, a workaholic father is an injury."

Robert Bly

1. What were the messages about who you are that you received from your dad by what he said, didn't say and how he acted towards you?

2. How do you think not receiving enough blessings from your father has impacted your life?

3. How have you dealt with the grief that you carry from missing a deeper connection with your father (your father wound)?

4. What are some things you wish you had had more time to do and share with your father?

7 | Our unhealed father wounds impact our entire lives.

"I am poor and needy and my heart is wounded within me."

Psalms, 109:22

"The task of healing is to respect oneself as a creature, no more and no less."

Wendell Berry

"If we do not transform our pain, we will most assuredly transmit it."

Richard Rohr

1. What kinds of behaviors have you developed to hide your grief from not having experienced enough of your father's blessings?

2. How has your unhealed grief influenced how you treat others?

   a. Your family

   b. Your wife

   c. Your co-workers

   d. Strangers you encounter in daily life

3. How has your grief from your 'father wound' impacted:

    a. Your body

    b. Your levels of stress

    c. Your spirit

4. What kinds of behaviors have you developed to hide your grief from not having experienced enough of your father's blessings?

5. How has your unhealed grief influenced how you treat others?
    a. Your family

    b. Your wife

    c. Your co-workers

    d. Strangers you encounter in daily life

6. How has your grief from your 'father wound' impacted:
    a. Your body

    b. Your levels of stress

    c. Your spirit

7. What other loses and relationships do you still need to grieve?

We need to wake up to how our wounds can be a gift, a journey from death to life.

The Wind One Brilliant Day

"The wind, one brilliant day, called to my soul with an odor of jasmine. 'In return for the odor of my jasmine, I'd like all the odor of your roses.' 'I have no roses; all the flowers in my garden are dead.' 'Well then, I'll take the withered petals and the yellow leaves and the waters of the fountain.' The wind left. And I wept. And I said to myself: 'What have you done with the garden that was entrusted to you'?"

Antonio Machado

1. What positive and negative, spoken and unspoken messages did you pick up about yourself from your family, your school mates and friends?

2. How did your struggles while growing up to fit in and to compete help you become the person you are today?

3. In what ways have you used your sadness and grief to create something positive in your life?

"You don't choose your family. They are God's gift to you, as you are to them."

Desmond Tutu

"The happiest moments of my life have been the few which I have passed at home in the bosom of my family."

Thomas Jefferson

1. What are some of your favorite memories of your family as a child?

2. What were some of the difficulties growing up in your family? What role did you play?

3. List one or two qualities or talents you appreciate about each of your family members, including your mom and dad.

4. What qualities and talents and accomplishments of yours do you trace directly back to your family?

10 Our lives are forever shaped by not being formally initiated by the older men in our communities.

"Initiation: the boy is brought into the 'new male womb,' the men's community where he would for months or years listen to the stories, learn the encyclopedia of the male culture, and wrestle with life questions of destiny and how men are."

Sam Keen

"An uninitiated man lives in an isolated body and a disconnected world. He must take personal responsibility for creating all the patterns and making all the connections, if there are any. It is an un-whole, incoherent, and finally unsafe world."

Richard Rohr

1. What were some of the privileges, responsibilities, risks and adventures that marked your journey from adolescents into manhood?

2. When did you move out of your childhood home, how old were you and what were some key experiences and feelings from that time?

3. After leaving home, what informal rituals of initiation, hazing, apprenticeship did you go through?

    a. 1st jobs

    b. College/tech schools

    c. Military

    d. Other

4. Who were some of the older men in your life you consider to have been mentors and wisdom figures during that time?

5. What were some life lessons you learned during those years?

"I love you without knowing how, or when, or from where. I love you simply, without problems or pride: I love you in this way because I do not know any other way of loving but this, in which there is no I or you, so intimate that your hand upon my chest is my hand, so intimate that when I fall asleep your eyes close."

Pablo Neruda

1. What were some of the high point and struggles on your journey that taught you about intimacy and love with women?

2. If you are married, what was it about the woman you married that drew you to her?

3. If you have children, how has each one been a blessing in your life and what is your wish for them?

4. If you have grandchildren, what stands out about each of them and what is a wish you have for each of them?

"There are two questions a man must ask himself. The first is 'where am I going?' and the second is 'who is willing to go with me?' If you ever get these questions in wrong order, you are in trouble."

Sam Keen

"In the sweetness of friendship let there be laughter, and sharing of pleasures. For in the dew of little things the heart finds its morning and is refreshed."

Kahlil Gibran

1. Who were some of your best childhood male friends and what did you enjoy the most about each of them?

2. Who are some of the male friends you have or had as a teen and as an adult?

3. When have you felt most lonely in your adult life?

4. What do male friendships offer you that you cannot always find in a relationship with a woman?

5. What are some of your best memories of going on adventures with your male friend(s)?

6. Who are some of the most important male friends in your life right now?

"We can't live for ourselves. A thousand fibers connect us with our fellow men; and among those fibers, as sympathetic threads, our actions run as causes, and they come back to us as effects."

Herman Melville

1. As a child what groups, sports teams and organizations did you belong to?

     a. Which ones meant the most to you?
     b. What was the 'price' of acceptance into these
       groups?

2. As a teen and young adult what groups, teams, organizations, etc. that you belonged to mean the most and why?

3. What group of kids in your school life were most threatening to you?

4. What groups of kids did you most want to belong to but were not accepted?

5. As an adult, what groups, organizations, communities do you belong to and value the most?

6. How does your belonging to these groups impact your spirit and help shape the direction of your life?

"Legionary life is beautiful, not because of riches, partying or the acquisition of luxury, but because of the noble comradeship which binds all Legionaries in a sacred brotherhood of struggle."

Corneliu Zelea Codreanu

1. What questionable behaviors did you go along with in order to belong to a group/gang/clique/team/organization?

2. What have been some of the greatest 'highs,' bonding moments, that you have had as a member of a group/gang/clique/team/organization?

3. What have been some of the greatest moments of sadness and loss that you have experienced by being a member of a particular group/gang/clique/team/organization?

4. What group or organization of men have you belonged to that you knew you would be willing to die for?

5. Describe a current group of males that you hang out with and what this group gives you?

15 Our spirits are fed through our music, our work and creativity.

"A man should hear a little music, read a little poetry, and see a fine picture every day of his life, in order that worldly cares may not obliterate the sense of the beautiful which God has implanted in the human soul."

Johann Wolfgang von Goethe

"We are creators at our very core. Only creating can make us happy, for in creating we tap into the deepest powers of self and universe and Divine Self."

Mathew Fox

1. As a child what were some ways that you expressed your creativity?

2. Who were some of the people in your life as a child who encouraged you to be creative?

3. What sports, arts, experiences in the outdoors, hobbies, etc., give you an outlet for your creativity?

4. What jobs in your life have you had the greatest opportunities to be creative?

5. In what ways do you believe God is using your creativity, gifts and talents to impact our world today?

6. List some of the music groups, performers, songs that have defined your life so far:

    a. As a teen

    b. As a young adult

    c. In your adult life

7. In what ways do you express gratitude to the Creator for all the talents and opportunities you have been given?

"The grand point is not to wear the garb, nor use the brogue of religion, but to process the life of God within, and feel and think as Jesus would have done because of that inner life. Small is the value of extended religion, unless it is the outcome of a life within."

C.S. Lewis

Every Foot a Shrine

"Every creature has a religion. Every foot is a shrine where a secret candle burns. Every cell in us worships God. Every arrow in the bow of desire has rushed out in hope of nearing Him."

Thomas Aquinas

1. As a child, what were some of your strongest memories of going to church?

2. As a child, how did your participation in an organized religion shape your beliefs about:

    a. God

    b. Heaven and hell and life after death

    c. Sin, punishment and mercy

    d. Our purpose for being born

3. How did your attitudes and beliefs change as you went through your adolescent years?

4. What have you come to believe today?

    a. God

    b. Heaven and hell and life after death

    c. Sin, punishment and mercy

    d. Our purpose for being born

5. What denomination do you identify with, if any?

6. How does organized religion impact your sense of purpose and meaning?

7. In what ways does organized religion enrich your spirituality today?

"For my part, I travel not to go anywhere, but to go. I travel for travel's sake. The great affair is to move."

Robert Louis Stevenson

"Twenty years from now you will be more disappointed by the things that you didn't do than by the ones you did do. So throw off the bowlines. Sail away from the safe harbor. Catch the trade winds in your sails. Explore. Dream. Discover."

Mark Twain

1. As child how did you respond to the inborn drive to seek out adventures in your world?

2. As a teen how did you respond to the 'inborn' drive to seek out adventures in your world?

3. What and who most impacted you about 'playing it safe' and resisting the drive for more adventure in your life?

4. What are some of your favorite memories of adventures you have shared with other men?

5. What are some of the goals and values other men in your life seek and take risks to attain?

6. What kinds of small and large adventures in your life today impact your spirituality in the deepest ways?

7. Write a first person message to yourself about the different adventures that you still feel drawn to in your life and what you will do to pursue them.

The Breeze At Dawn

"The breeze at dawn has secrets to tell you. Don't go back to sleep. You must ask for what you really want. Don't go back to sleep. People are going back and forth across the doorsill where the two worlds touch. The door is round and open. Don't go back to sleep."

Rumi

1. Have you ever had an ongoing, deep within sense that you are a beloved son of God?

2. Describe a time in nature when you were alone and felt some level of oneness with the source of all life.

3. What are some of the distractions, bad habits and daily routines as a teen that kept you from living fully in the moment and feeling alive and content?

4. Today, what are some of the family, work related and relationship distractions that keep you from living fully in the moment and feeling alive and content?

19 In Nature we are drawn into the great mysteries of life.

"My profession is always to be alert, to find God in nature, to know God's lurking places, to attend to all the oratorios and the operas in nature.

Henry David Thoreau

"My father considered a walk among the mountains as the equivalent of churchgoing."

Aldous Huxley

1. What are some of the miracles of nature that have taught you about the endless creativity and generosity of our Creator?

2. What are some of your favorite sights, sounds, smells, etc. of the 4 seasons?

   a. Fall

   b. Winter

   c. Spring

   d. Summer

3. Write a poem or short prayer/litany expressing your gratitude for the joy and wonder you have experienced in nature.

20 In nature we are brought into right relationship with our place in the universe.

"How hard to realize that every camp of men or beast has this glorious starry firmament for a roof! In such places standing alone on the mountain-top it is easy to realize that whatever special nests we make - leaves and moss like the marmots and birds, or tents or piled stone - we all dwell in a house of one room - the world with the firmament for its roof - and are sailing the celestial spaces without leaving any track."

John Muir

20

1. Describe an experience in nature where you felt overwhelmed by the vastness of the universe.

2. Describe your feelings and how your senses were awakened when:

    a. You stood on a mountain top.

    b. You stood on the shore of a lake or ocean and watched the sun go down.

    c. You were swallowed up in a mist coming off a river, mountain, storm.

3. What are some of the great unsolved mysteries of the universe that you are amazed by and wonder about?

21 When we are awake we experience eternity now, on earth as it is in heaven.

"Heaven is under our feet as well as over our heads."

Henry David Thoreau

"He proclaimed the good news, the reign of God is here"

Mark, 1:15

1. Describe times as a child when you experienced heaven on earth:

    a. In nature and the change of seasons.

    b. In moments of play.

    c. In experiences of work.

    d. In moments of creativity.

2. Describe times as an adult when you experienced heaven on earth:

    a. In nature and the change of seasons.

    b. In moments of play.

    c. In experiences of work.

    d. In moments of creativity.

    e. When you experienced being loved and loving others.

We all have a deep inner knowing that our true selves are designed to be mystics.

Has My Heart Gone To Sleep?

"Has my heart gone to sleep? Have the beehives of my dreams stopped working, the waterwheel of the mind run dry, scoops turning empty, only shadow inside? No, my heart is not asleep. It is awake, wide awake. Not asleep, not dreaming — its eyes are opened wide watching distant signals, listening on the rim of vast silence."

Antonio Machado

1. Describe a time when you welled up with tears of joy by sharing in someone else's happiness.

2. Describe a time when you welled up with tears of sadness as you shared in the pain of someone else.

3. When are you most aware of being connected to all people, no matter their religion, race, economic background, etc. because of our shared humanity?

4. Describe a situation where you were able to understand and have compassion for someone who has acted out violence towards others.

5. Describe a time when you felt gratitude in the midst of great suffering and loss.

6. What messages in the male culture about being a man keeps you from acknowledging your inner mystic?

"Apprehend God in all things, for God is in all things. Every single creature is full of God and is a book about God. Every creature is a word of God."

Meister Eckhart

1. Describe something very small in nature that expresses your sense of gratitude for the creativity of our Creator:

2. Describe something very large in nature that expresses your sense of gratitude for the creativity of our creator:

3. What do your experiences of wonder and gratitude in nature reveal to you about the nature and mystery of our Creator God?

4. How do you see the intersection of a God who creates all that is with the scientific discoveries associated with evolution.

The Road Not Taken by Robert Frost

Two roads diverged in a yellow wood,
And sorry I could not travel both
And be one traveler, long I stood
And looked down one as far as I could
To where it bent in the undergrowth;

Then took the other, as just as fair,
And having perhaps the better claim
Because it was grassy and wanted wear,
Though as for that the passing there
Had worn them really about the same,

And both that morning equally lay
In leaves no step had trodden black.
Oh, I kept the first for another day!
Yet knowing how way leads on to way
I doubted if I should ever come back.

I shall be telling this with a sigh
Somewhere ages and ages hence:
Two roads diverged in a wood, and I -,
I took the one less traveled by,
And that has made all the difference.

1. Describe an experience when you felt at one, at peace with the mystery of life:

    a. In nature

    b. In a relationship

    c. In a moment of creativity

    d. In a moment when your body felt most alive

3. Describe a woods where you have often been drawn to, where you have gone to sort out your life.

4. What was one road less traveled that you have taken and the impact it has had on your life?

"Inside this new love, die. Your way begins on the other side. Become the sky. Take an axe to the prison wall. Escape. Walk out like somebody suddenly born into color. Do it now. You're covered with thick cloud. Slide out the side. Die, and be quiet. Quietness is the surest sign that you've died. Your old life was a frantic running from silence. The speechless full moon comes out now."

Rumi

1. When and where as a child did you experience silence and enjoy it?

2. What daily and/or somewhat regular practices do you use to rest in the quiet of the present moment? Meditation, reading, yoga, centering prayer, walks, retreats, tai-chi, running, at the gym etc.

3. What habits and experiences will you develop as a pathway to finding room for more quiet and solitude in your life?

"You must learn an inner solitude, wherever or with whomsoever you may be. You must learn to penetrate things and find God there, to get a strong impression of God firmly fixed in your mind."

Meister Eckhart

1. As a child and teen when and where did you most often feel 'lonely'?

2. As an adult when and where do you most often feel 'lonely'?

3. What disciplines and habits do you use to find more alone time and solitude in your life?

4. In your life adventures and when you have been alone with yourself at home or in nature what have you sensed, learned about who this God is that loves you?

The Winter of Listening

"The fire is the main comfort of the camp, whether in summer or winter, and is about as ample at one season as at another. It is as well for cheerfulness as for warmth and dryness."

Henry David Thoreau

"You, darkness, that I came from, I love you more that all the fires that fence in the world, for the fire makes a circle of light for everyone and then no one outside learns of you. But the darkness pulls in everything — shapes and fires, animals and myself, how easily it gathers them — powers and people — and it is possible — a great presence is moving near me. I have faith in the nights."

Reiner Maria Rilke

1. As a child and teen what did you like the most about hanging out around 'camp fires'?

2. Where and when did you most often experience sitting around camp fires?

3. When and where have you experienced 'being swallowed up' by the power and darkness of the night sky?

4. How has being alone in nature, surrounded by the darkness and the power of nature helped you confront your 'mortality'?

5. Imagine yourself sitting around a campfire late at night, with a brilliant, star studded sky overhead, look around your campfire, who is there with you?

Look each one in the eyes and share a nod of acknowledgment with each one.

"I have come that you may have life, life in an abundance."

John, 10:10

Today Like Every Other Day

"Today, like every other day, we wake up empty and frightened. Don't open the door to the study and begin reading. Take down the dulcimer. Let the beauty we love be what we do. There are hundreds of ways to kneel and kiss the ground."

Rumi

28

1. How does your love of life most often show up in how you live your daily life?

2. How have you dealt with depression and or emotional crises in your life?

3. In what ways do you expose yourself to beauty?:

    a. In the arts

    b. In nature:

    c. In your work:

    d. In your family:

    e. In your friendships:

4. How will you make more time to enjoy what you consider to be 'beauty' in your life?

29 Our spirits are healed when we take time to heal our bodies.

"Fly-fishers are usually brain-workers in society. Along the banks of purling streams, beneath the shadows of umbrageous trees, or in the secluded nooks of charming lakes, they have ever been found, drinking deep of the invigorating forces of nature - giving rest and tone to over-taxed brains and wearied nerves - while gracefully wielding the supple rod, the invisible leader, and the fairy-like fly."

James Henshall

"If fishing is a religion, fly fishing is high church. "

James Henshall

29

1. What memories do you have of fishing as a child and teen?

2. What was it about the experiences of fishing as a child and teen that have left the most vivid memories?

3. As an adult, what is it about fishing that makes you feel most alive?

4. If fishing isn't your sport, what activity in nature overwhelms you to the point where you leave all your worries and cares behind?

Love After Love

"The time will come when, with elation you will greet yourself arriving at your own door, in your own mirror and each will smile at the other's welcome, and say, sit here. Eat. You will love again the stranger who was your self. Give wine. Give bread. Give back your heart to itself, to the stranger who has loved you all your life, whom you ignored for another, who knows you by heart. Take down the love letters from the bookshelf, the photographs, the desperate notes, peel your own image from the mirror. Sit. Feast on your life."

Derek Walcott

1. Wherever you are on your journey right now, how would you answer:

    a. I am

    b. I am

    c. I am

2. To what extent are you able to accept that you carry deep within you, woven into your very DNA, the divine indwelling of the Creator of all that exists?

3. What are the positive, self-affirming messages you need to repeat over and over to yourself?

4. As an adult, to what extent are you able to embrace your 'broken' self and your 'best self' as the sum of your 'true self'?

5. How would the people in your life right now describe your best qualities?

"Last night as I was sleeping, I dreamt—marvelous error!—that I had a beehive here inside my heart. And the golden bees were making white combs and sweet honey from my old failures. Last night as I was sleeping, I dreamt—marvelous error!—that a fiery sun was giving light inside my heart. It was fiery because I felt warmth as from a hearth, and sun because it gave light and brought tears to my eyes. Last night as I slept, I dreamt—marvelous error!—that it was God I had here inside my heart."

Antonio Machado

1. Who in your life has been a 'source of redemption' because of the way they have forgiven you?

2. What life experiences have 'broken your sprit' and eventually became a source of growth and personal transformation?

3. What experiences in your life have taught you to accept things as they are and that you can't control life events?

4. How will you acknowledge your brokenness and accept that your God wraps you in a 'blanket of unconditional love'?

"Male saints are, quite simply, people who are whole. They trust their masculine soul because they have met the good masculine side of God, whom we have called 'The Father'. They do not need to affirm or deny, judge or ignore. But they are free to do all of them with impunity. A saint is invincible."

Richard Rohr

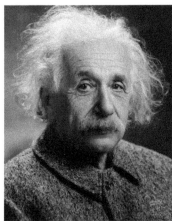

1. Based on Richard Rohr's definition of a saint, who are the men you have known in your life who best fit this definition:

    a. Men you have personally known:

    b. Men in history who are examples of this 'saint' definition:

2. What are some of the best qualities that describe for you what it means to be a 'saint', the best of what it means to be masculine, today?

3. What qualities do you want to nurture in your own life on your journey to being 'a saint'?

4. In what ways do you show a generous and grateful spirit to those you encounter in your life every day?

33 We learn to care for our spirits by taking care of our physical selves.

"The great malady of the 20th century, affecting us individually and socially, is a 'loss of soul'. When soul is neglected, it just doesn't go away; it appears symptomatically in obsession, addictions, violence, loss of meaning."

Thomas Moore

The Time Before Death

"Friend, hope for the Guest while you are alive.
Jump into experience while you are alive! Think... and think... while you are alive. What you call "salvation" belongs to the time before death."

Kabir

1. In what ways have you kept yourself busy and distracted that keeps you from attending to the health of your 'soul'?

2. What are some of the habits, the arts, the work, the quiet, the foods and physical disciplines, etc. you use to feed your spirit and fill your soul?

3. How does your soul best express itself in the outside world around you?

"When he saw the crowds, he had compassion for them, because they were harassed and helpless, like sheep without a shepherd."

Matthew, 9:36

"I have a dream that my four children will one day live in a nation where they will not be judged by the color of their skin but by the content of their character."

Martin Luther King

1. What are situations in your life where you most often feel connected in some way with individuals and groups who are oppressed and mistreated in some way?

2. In your everyday life who are 'your neighbors' who you are aware of needing to be 'lifted up' in some way?

3. In what ways are you willing to stand up on behalf of women who are treated as less than full, equal members of our society?

4. Who are some males you admire for the way they sacrifice their lives on behalf of those who are hurting and being mistreated in some way?

"I have always found that mercy bears richer fruits than strict justice."

Abraham Lincoln

"We are called to seek mercy, act justly and walk humbly with our God."

Micah, 6:8

1. Who are the people in your life who have shown you mercy?

2. What are some ways you have reached out to serve those in need?

3. How do you see yourself being more active in helping your 'neighbor in need'?

4. What are some ways you will mentor young boys and men by your example on behalf of those in our communities who are in need in some way?

We are most alive when we shake off the burden of obligations and look for the enchantment imbedded in everyday life.

Escape

"Life is when we get out of the glass bottles of our own ego, and when we escape like squirrels from turning in the cages of our personality and get into the forest again, we shall shiver with cold and fright but things will happen to us so that we don't know ourselves. Cool, un-lying life will rush in, and passion will make our bodies taut with power, we shall stamp our feet with new power and old things will fall down, we shall laugh, and institutions will curl up like burnt paper."

DH Lawrence

1. Describe in detail a favorite place in nature that saturates your senses and wakes you up to the 'present moment'.

2. When have you recently felt so alive and at home with nature that you spontaneously broke out in laughter or tears?

3. Looking back over your life, what are some 'life lessons' you have learned while working, playing and being in nature?

Our greatest longing is to live in union with the fierce and loving source of all creation — God.

"He's wild, you know."

C.S. Lewis

"It's in Mystery that we live, move and have our being."

Acts 17:28

The Essence of Desire

"I did not have to ask my heart what it wanted, because of all the desires I have ever known just one thing did I cling to for it was the essence of all desire: to hold beauty in my soul's arms."

John of the Cross

1. In what ways have you experienced God as being 'wild'?

   a. In nature.

   b. In relationships.

   c. In the interconnectedness of all creation.

   d. In your deepest self, knowing the 'Source of all life' is woven into your DNA and that you are loved.

2. How much do you relate to the notion of God as being ultimately a Mystery, beyond knowing by our limited human abilities?

3. How aware are you of a 'deep, inner longing' to love and be loved by God who is ultimately a 'mystery'?

4. How able are you to relate to a God who is a mysterious, all loving, presence who fills the universe with love and creativity?

"Just to be is a blessing. Just to live is a miracle."

Rabbi Heschel

From My Breath

"From My Breath I extract God. And my eye is a shop where I offer Him to the world."

Thomas Aquinas

I Live My Life

"I live my life in widening circles that reach out across the world. I may not complete this last one but I give myself to it. I circle around God, around the primordial tower. I've been circling for thousands of years and I still don't know: am I a falcon, a storm, or a great song?"

Rainer Maria Rilke

1. How often do you reflect on your mortality and what are some of your greatest fears and questions about dying?

2. What do you believe about 'life after death'?

3. How do you want to be remembered after you die?

4. Name those closest to you who you are grateful for right now in your life.

5. What are some of your life experiences that you are most grateful for.

5. In what ways does thinking about your mortality motivate you to live your daily life?

Allen, G., Williams, P., Rusaw, R. (2006). When I'm Learning to Love. Standard Publishing.

Armstrong, B. (2006). Musings from the Mountaintop. Xulon Press.

Berry, W. (2010). What are people for?: Essays. Counterpoint Press.

Bly, R. (2015). Iron John: A book about men. Da Capo Press.

Bly, R. (1981). Selected poems of Rainer Maria Rilke. New York: Harper & Row.

Codreanu, C. Z. For my legionaries: The Iron Guard. Black House Pbulishing

Creamer, Kenneth. (2013). The Reformation of Union State Sovereignty: The Path Back to the Political System Our Founding Fathers Intended — A Sovereign Life, Liberty, and a Free. iUniverse, Inc.

Easwaran, Eknath. (2010). Words to Live By: Daily Inspiration for Spiritual Living. Nilgiri Press.

Fehrenbacher, D., & Fehrenbacher, V. (Eds.). (1996). Recollected Words of Abraham Lincoln. Stanford University Press.

Fox, M. (2004). Creativity. Penguin.

Fox, M. (2010). The hidden spirituality of men: Ten metaphors to awaken the sacred masculine. New World Library.

Fox, M. (Ed.). (1983). Meditations with Meister Eckhart. Simon and Schuster.

Frost, R. (1921). Mountain Interval. H. Holt.

Gibran, K. (2012). The Prophet. Oneworld Publications.

Harvey, A. (1996). Light upon light: inspirations from Rumi. North Atlantic Books.

Henshall, J. A. (1920). Book of the black bass. Stewart & Kidd.

Heschel, A. J. (1996). Moral grandeur and spiritual audacity: Essays. Macmillan.

Hughes, T. O. (2012). Finding hope and meaning in suffering. SPCK.

James, S., & Thomas, D. (2011). Wild things: The art of nurturing boys. Tyndale House Publishers, Inc.

Keen, S. (2010). Fire in the belly: On being a man. Bantam.

Ladinsky, D. (Ed.). (2002). Love poems from God: Twelve sacred voices from the East and West. Penguin.

Landauer, Mary Linda. (2007). When Water Runs Uphill. AuthorHouse.

Lawrence, D. H. (1977). The Complete Poems, ed. Vivian de Sola Pinto and Warren Roberts. Penguin Books.

Machado, A. (1983). Times alone: selected poems of Antonio Machado. Wesleyan University Press.

Machado, A., & Trueblood, A. S. (1988). Antonio Machado: Selected Poems. Harvard University Press.

Moore, T., & Roberts, H. (1992). Care of the soul: A guide for cultivating depth and sacredness in everyday life. HarperCollins.

Moyers, B. D. (1990). A world of ideas II: Public opinions from private citizens (Vol. 2). Main Street Books.

Neruda, P. (1975). Twenty Love Poems and a Song of Despair, trans. WS Merwin. London: Jonathan Cape.

Nisker, W., & Nisker, S. (1990). Crazy wisdom. Ten Speed Press.

Pew Research Center (2018). Being Christian in Western Europe. In The Pew Forum on Religion & Public Life.

Pew Research Center. (2012). "Nones" on the rise: One-in-five adults have no religious affiliation. In The Pew Forum on Religion & Public Life.

Rapanos, George. (2006). The Tao of Religion: The Eternal Harmony of Opposites — Judaism, Christianity and Islam's Handbook to Eastern Spirituality. Avensblume Press.

Radford, Michael. (2004). A Salute to Service: The Rebirth of Patriotism. New Leaf Press.

Rilke, R. M. (2005). Rilke's book of hours: Love poems to God. Penguin.

Roberts, Dale L. (2015). Motivational Quotations Box Set: 646 Inspirational Quotes to Uplift, Motivate & Empower You. One Jacked Monkey.

Rohr, R., & Martos, J. (2005). From wild man to wise man: Reflections on male spirituality. Franciscan Media.

Rohr, R. (2016). Things hidden: Scripture as spirituality. Franciscan Media.

Rumi, J. A. D., & Barks, C. (1995). The Essential Rumi. Penguin.

Spangler, D. (2000). Parent as Mystic, Mystic as Parent. Penguin.

Stevenson, R. L. (2014). The Cevennes journal: notes on a journey through the French highlands. Random House.

Sutter, Trista. (2013). Happily Ever After: the Life Changing Power of a Grateful Heart. Hachette Press.

Thoreau, H. D. (2014). The Maine Woods: A fully annotated edition. Yale University Press.

Thoreau, H. D., (2016). Walden, Or, Life in the Woods. Wisehouse Classics

Thoreau, H. D., Torrey, B., & Sanborn, F. B. (1906). The Writings of Henry David Thoreau (Vol. 20). Houghton, Mifflin.

Teale, E. W. (1954). Wilderness World of John Muir. Houghton Mifflin.

Tutu, D. (2011). God has a dream: A vision of hope for our times. Random House.

Walcott, D. (1986). Collected Poems, 1948-1984. Macmillan.

White, W. L. (2009). The image of man in CS Lewis. Wipf and Stock Publishers.

Photos

Photos were selected from www.pexels.com and www.pixabay.com and are available for personal and commercial use without the need for attribution.

"It's hard to understand complex licenses that is why all photos on Pexels are licensed under the Creative Commons Zero (CC0) license. This means the pictures are completely free to be used for any legal purpose.

- The pictures are free for personal and even for commercial use.
- You can modify, copy and distribute the photos.
- All without asking for permission or setting a link to the source. So, attribution is not required.

The only restriction is that identifiable people may not appear in a bad light or in a way that they may find offensive, unless they give their consent. You should also make sure the depicted content (people, logos, private property, etc.) is suitable for your application and doesn't infringe any rights.

The CC0 license was released by the non-profit organization Creative Commons (CC)."

You can use all images and videos published on Pixabay for free (except as set out below). You may use them for commercial and non-commercial purposes, in altered and unaltered form. You don't need to ask permission from or provide credit to the image author or Pixabay, although it is appreciated when possible.

From the Author

When I was growing up, there was never any distinction between the realm of spirituality and organized religion. They were considered one in the same. Today most surveys tracking the religious affiliations of men have choices of: 'religious, 'religious and spiritual', 'not religious', 'spiritual but not religious' and 'none'. For a very long time men who rejected organized religion or hung around on the edges were considered to not be spiritual. For many men organized religion was and still is considered to be 'boring', too feminine, not relevant, and not connecting with their deepest spiritual hungers.

In a very broad sense, the male journey is a 'spiritual journey'. At their best self, men are deeply passionate about finding meaning and purpose for their lives. They are often misled and get lost on this journey but at their core they long to love, be loved and to make a difference that will last long after they are gone. This journal is for helping men 'wake up' to their true 'spiritual' selves.

Steve Robach
612-322-3602
steverobach11@gmail.com

CPSIA information can be obtained
at www.ICGtesting.com
Printed in the USA
LVHW020550270819
629004LV00002B/2/P

9 781977 206817